jBIO
MOZART

03/25/15

Loria, Laura

Wolfgang Amadeus Mozart:
Musical prodigy and composer
CHILDREN

BRITANNICA BEGINNER BIOS

WOLFGANG AMADEUS MOZART

MUSICAL PRODIGY AND COMPOSER

LAURA LORIA

Britannica®
Educational Publishing

IN ASSOCIATION WITH

ROSEN
EDUCATIONAL SERVICES

Published in 2015 by Britannica Educational Publishing (a trademark of Encyclopædia Britannica, Inc.) in association with The Rosen Publishing Group, Inc.
29 East 21st Street, New York, NY 10010

Distributed exclusively by Rosen Publishing.
To see additional Britannica Educational Publishing titles, go to rosenpublishing.com.

First Edition

Britannica Educational Publishing
J. E. Luebering: Director, Core Reference Group
Mary Rose McCudden: Editor, Britannica Student Encyclopedia

Rosen Publishing
Executive Editor: Hope Killcoyne
Editor: Jeanne Nagle
Nelson Sá: Art Director
Designer: Nicole Russo
Photography Manager: Cindy Reiman

Library of Congress Cataloging-in-Publication Data

Loria, Laura.
Wolfgang Amadeus Mozart/Laura Loria.
        pages cm.—(Britannica beginner bios)
Includes bibliographical references and index.
ISBN 978-1-62275-681-0 (library bound)—ISBN 978-1-62275-682-7 (pbk.)—ISBN 978-1-62275-683-4 (6-pack)
1. Mozart, Wolfgang Amadeus, 1756-1791—Juvenile literature. 2. Composers—Austria—Biography—Juvenile literature. I. Title.
ML3930.M9L67 2015
780.92—dc23
[B]
                                                                                2014023248

Manufactured in the United States of America

Cover Imagno/Hulton Fine Art Collection/Getty Images; p. 1, interior pages background © iStockphoto.com/AlexStar; p. 4 Derek Latta/Shutterstock.com; p. 5 Markus Lange/Robert Harding World Imagery/Getty Images; p. 6 Hiroyuki Ito/Hulton Archive/Getty Images p. 8 Martin Schalk/Getty Images/Thinkstock; p. 9 Photos.com/Jupiterimages; p. 10 From the National Trust Property, Fenton House, Hampstead, London; by gracious permission of Her Majesty Queen Elizabeth, the Queen Mother; p. 11 Photos.com/Thinkstock; p. 12 Print Collector/Hulton Archive/Getty Images; pp. 13, 16, 18, 21, 26 DEA/A. Dagli Orti/De Agostini/Getty Images; p. 14 DEA/G. Dagli Orti/De Agostini/Getty Images; p. 15 (top) SuperStock; p. 15 (bottom) Encyclopædia Britannica, Inc.; p 20 © AP Images; p. 22 Dieter Nagl/AFP/Getty Images; p. 24 Erich Lessing/Art Resource, NY; p. 25 © Orion/courtesy Everett Collection.

CONTENTS

CHAPTER ONE

MUSIC YESTERDAY AND TODAY

When you listen to the radio or watch television, you can hear many different kinds of music. You can hear and see your favorite performers singing and playing instruments. You can also buy their music on CD or download the music to

Listening to music through earphones can be a lot of fun.

Wolfgang Amadeus Mozart wrote music in the 1700s. People still listen to his music today.

Quick Fact

As a young boy, Mozart was afraid of the trumpet.

MOZART

an electronic device. You might like rock, pop, or hip-hop. There are many different kinds of music today.

Now imagine that you lived more than 200 years ago, in the late 1700s. What kind of music would you have listened to? Where would you have heard it? If you lived in Europe, you would have gone to private concerts or to church to hear music. The type of music you would have heard is now called

This string quartet is playing classical music. A string quartet is a group of four musicians who play stringed instruments.

CLASSICAL MUSIC. Classical music is complex. It can be played on a single instrument or using a combination of many instruments. Those instruments can include violins, pianos, flutes, and trumpets.

Vocabulary Box

CLASSICAL MUSIC is formal music that is written as a piece of art, not just to entertain. It has strict rules and is played exactly as it is written.

The music stars of the 1700s were not the musicians. The composers, who wrote the music, were the stars. People would attend concerts because they liked the music of the composer. Wealthy people would hire composers whom they liked to write music for them.

One of the most famous composers of classical music was Wolfgang Amadeus Mozart. He wrote more than 600 pieces of music. His music is still played all around the world.

CHAPTER TWO

YOUNG MOZART

Mozart was born on January 27, 1756, in the city of Salzburg, in what is today Austria. His full name was Johann Chrysostom Wolfgang Amadeus Mozart. However, he is generally known as Wolfgang

The house where Mozart was born still stands in Austria today.

Quick Fact

Mozart's nickname was Wolferl. His sister's nickname was Nannerl.

Amadeus Mozart today. His father, Leopold, was a musician. He wrote a famous book about how to play the violin. Leopold and his wife, Anna

This painting shows Mozart (center) with his sister and father. A portrait of his mother hangs on the wall.

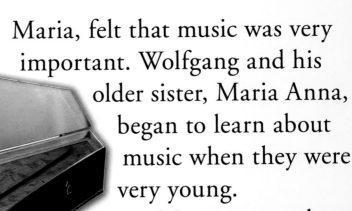

Maria, felt that music was very important. Wolfgang and his older sister, Maria Anna, began to learn about music when they were very young.

Mozart was only three years old when he began playing the harpsichord, which is like a piano. By the time he was five years old, he was writing his own music. He could play many different instruments. Mozart was known as a child **PRODIGY**.

Leopold wanted to show everyone how gifted his children

A harpsichord is a keyboard instrument in which strings are set in vibration by plucking.

Vocabulary Box
A **PRODIGY** is someone who is unusually talented.

A portrait shows Mozart as a young child.

Mozart often performed with his father and sister when he was a boy.

were. In 1763 the Mozart family went on a tour of the musical centers of western Europe. Mozart and his sister played music in royal courts and churches in many different cities. The cities included Vienna, Austria; Paris, France; and London, England. While traveling, Mozart continued to write music and to learn different styles of music. It was during this trip that Mozart's first music was published. He was just eight years old at the time! It was the beginning of a very productive musical career. The family returned to Salzburg in 1766.

CHAPTER THREE

TOURING

In 1767 the Mozart family left Salzburg again, this time for a long stay in Vienna. Mozart continued to learn and write new styles of music. He wrote his first OPERA, called *La finta semplice* (The Feigned Simpleton), in 1768. He had hoped that it would be performed in Vienna, but the

This is how the city of Salzburg looked during Mozart's time.

Vocabulary Box

An **OPERA** is a play with music. All of the words are sung.

performance was cancelled. Mozart and his father were disappointed. However, the opera was staged in Salzburg in 1769.

That same year, Mozart and his father traveled to Italy. The young Mozart attended a music school in Bologna to learn more about writing operas. In October 1770 he earned the title of master composer. He performed in many other cities as well. For the next few years they traveled between Salzburg and Italy.

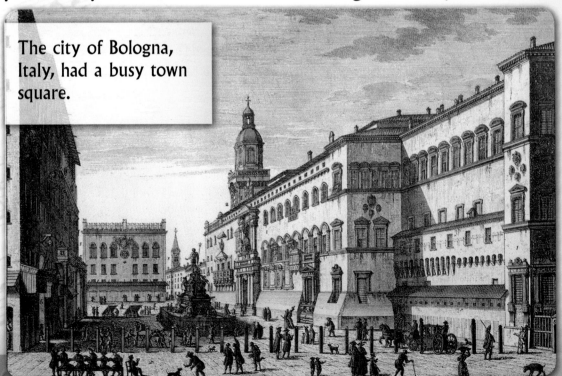

The city of Bologna, Italy, had a busy town square.

At age 15, Mozart spent a lot of time in Italy.

In Salzburg Mozart worked for the court orchestra. An orchestra is a group of musicians that plays works written for many instruments. Mozart played in the orchestra and wrote music for the orchestra to play. But after a while he

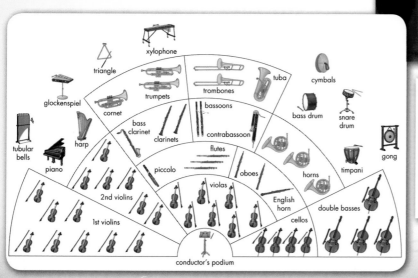

In an orchestra, the players are arranged according to the instruments they play.

Mozart clashed with Hieronymus von Colloredo, who became the archbishop of Salzburg in 1772.

wanted a chance to do more important work.

In 1778 Mozart and his mother went to Paris. There he

Quick Fact

One day when he was 12, Mozart heard a special piece of church music. Later that night, he wrote the whole thing from memory.

> **Vocabulary Box**
>
> A **SYMPHONY** is a long work that is written for many different instruments. Symphonies are played by orchestras.

continued to write music. His Paris **SYMPHONY** is considered to be one of his best symphonies. Sadly, his mother died shortly after it was first performed.

Mozart could not find a permanent job, so he returned home to work in Salzburg in 1780. He also kept writing operas and other works. They were performed in major cities throughout Europe. Mozart was not happy with the way he was treated at the court orchestra in Salzburg. He argued with his employer, the archbishop of Salzburg. In 1781 he finally left the orchestra and moved to Vienna.

CHAPTER FOUR

THE VIENNA YEARS

Constanze Weber was a singer. She came from a musical family.

In Vienna, Mozart stayed with family friends, the Webers. He fell in love with their daughter, Constanze. Mozart's father did not want him to marry Constanze, but the couple got married anyway in 1782.

Mozart's opera *Die Entführung*

aus dem Serail (The Abduction from the Seraglio) was performed in 1782. It is in a form of opera called singspiel. Singspiels have a mix of singing and speech. The Abduction from the Seraglio helped develop the singspiel style.

During this period, Mozart also gave music lessons and played the piano in concerts. At the time, concerts in Vienna were often held at the homes of rich families.

Mozart became very popular in Vienna. He was hired to write many pieces. He never seemed to earn enough money, though. Mozart and his family spent more money than he earned. So he was always looking for new **COMMISSIONS**.

Many of Mozart's most famous works were written during this time. He wrote

Vocabulary Box

COMMISSIONS are offers of money to create pieces of art. Commissions from rich people are how composers once earned a living.

This performance of *The Marriage of Figaro* took place more than 200 years after it was written.

symphonies, operas, and **CONCERTOS**. The opera *Le nozze di Figaro* (*The Marriage of Figaro*), from 1786, was a happy love story. It was very successful

Vocabulary Box

CONCERTOS are musical pieces featuring one particular instrument that plays along with the rest of the orchestra.

in Vienna. It was even more popular in the city of Prague. Mozart was so grateful to the people of Prague for their love of his music that he wrote a symphony for them. Mozart's opera *Don Giovanni* was performed for the first time in Prague as well.

Mozart also continued to write many types of music other than operas. The work called *Eine kleine Nachtmusik* contains one of his best-known melodies. The

Quick Fact

The theater director in Prague where *The Marriage of Figaro* was performed asked Mozart to write something specifically for Prague. That work was the opera *Don Giovanni.*

String quartets would entertain people in their homes during Mozart's time.

name of the piece means "a little night music." Its official name is the Serenade No. 13 in G Major. It was written as a chamber piece. This is a piece that

Unusual costumes help tell the fantastic story of *The Magic Flute.*

is played by a small group of musicians. *Eine kleine Nachtmusik* was written for two violins, a viola, a cello, and a double bass.

In 1787 Mozart's father died. That same year, Mozart was offered the job as official composer by Emperor Joseph II in Vienna. Mozart continued writing. His opera *Die Zauberflöte* (*The Magic Flute*) was first performed in 1791. The story is a fairy tale, featuring a noble prince, the beautiful young woman with whom he falls in love, and the bird-catcher who helps them. The opera was a hit. By that time, Mozart's health was not good. As he got sicker, though, he continued to write.

CHAPTER FIVE

THE LAST DAYS

The last music ever written by Mozart has been preserved.

Mozart died on December 5, 1791, at the age of 35. He was writing a **REQUIEM MASS** at the time. A student of his finished the requiem, based on Mozart's notes. It is one of his best known works.

Vocabulary Box

A REQUIEM MASS is religious music written for a funeral.

Actor Tom Hulce played Mozart in the movie *Amadeus*.

In 1980 a play called *Amadeus* was written about Mozart's life. It was later turned into a movie, which won many awards. The play was based on the composer's life, but it changed some of the events. It even included some events that did not really happen.

Composer Ludwig van Beethoven studied under Mozart. His music is equally famous.

Mozart was the most gifted composer of his time and one of the greatest composers to have ever lived. He liked to learn new styles and put them into his own creations. His music can be playful and silly, as well as thoughtful and serious. Composers who came after Mozart looked up to him because he was so original and creative.

> **Quick Fact**
>
> Lincoln Center in New York City hosts a series of concerts called the Mostly Mozart Festival every summer.

During his short life he composed more than 50 symphonies and 15 operas. He also wrote many works for choir, orchestra, and smaller groups of instruments. Although they are more than 200 years old, his compositions are still very popular.

Mozart's house in Salzburg is now a museum. The city also holds a music festival every year. Mozart's music is a major part of the festival.

TIMELINE

1756: Wolfgang Amadeus Mozart is born on January 27, in Salzburg, Austria.

1759: Mozart begins music lessons.

1761: Mozart begins composing music.

1763: The Mozart family begins its musical tours of Europe.

1764: Mozart publishes his first works in Paris.

1768: Mozart writes his first opera, *La finta semplice.*

1770: Mozart is named a master composer by the Philharmonic Academy in Bologna, Italy.

1773: Mozart writes six string quartets, symphonies, and a piano concerto in Vienna.

1775: Mozart begins a long period of work for the archbishop of Salzburg, writing mostly church music and shorter pieces.

1777: Unhappy with his job in Salzburg, Mozart gets permission from the archbishop to look for musical opportunities elsewhere.

1778: Mozart writes his Paris Symphony. Mozart's mother, Anna Maria, dies in Paris.

1781: Mozart leaves the royal orchestra in Salzburg and moves to Vienna.

1782: Mozart marries Constanze Weber.

1783: The finished sections of Mozart's *Mass in C Minor* are performed. Mozart's wife Constanze is one of the singers. The mass is left unfinished at Mozart's death.

1784: Mozart's first surviving son, Karl Thomas, is born.

1786: Mozart writes the opera *The Marriage of Figaro*.

1787: Mozart writes the opera *Don Giovanni* and his famous piece *Eine kleine Nachtmusik*.

1789: Mozart travels to Berlin, where he writes music, for piano and violin.

1790: Mozart's opera *Così fan tutte* premieres. It is performed only five times before the death of the emperor closes the theaters in Vienna.

1791: Mozart's second surviving son, Franz Xaver, is born.

1791: Mozart's opera *The Magic Flute* premieres.

1791: Mozart dies on December 5 from a long illness.

GLOSSARY

CANCELLED Caused something to end or not take place.

COMPOSER Someone who writes music.

COMPOSITIONS Written pieces of music, especially ones that are very long or complex.

CONCERTS Events at which people play music for others to listen to.

CREATIVE Having or showing an ability to make new things or think of new ideas.

INSTRUMENTS Devices that are used to make music.

MELODIES Series of notes that form the main tunes in a piece of music.

ORCHESTRA A group of musicians organized to play classical music together.

PRODUCTIVE Producing or able to produce something, especially in large amounts.

PUBLISHED Prepared and produced (a book, magazine, piece of music, or so forth) for sale.

BOOKS

Bailey, Gerry. *Mozart's Wig.* St. Catharines, ON, Canada: Crabtree Publishing Company, 2009.

Stanley, Diane. *Mozart: The Wonder Child: A Puppet Play in Three Acts.* New York, NY: Harper Collins, 2009.

Summerer, Eric. *Wolfgang Amadeus Mozart.* New York, NY: PowerKids Press, 2006.

Vernon, Roland. *Introducing Mozart.* New York, NY: Chelsea House Publishing, 2000.

Weeks, Marcus. *Mozart: The Boy Who Changed the World with His Music.* Des Moines, IA: National Geographic Children's Books, 2013.

WEBSITES

Because of the changing nature of Internet links, Rosen Publishing has developed an online list of websites related to the subject of this book. This site is updated regularly. Please use this link to access the list:

http://www.rosenlinks.com/BBB/Moz

INDEX